G000140325

I HATE YOU THE LEAST

summersdale

I HATE YOU THE LEAST

An Hachette UK Company
www.hachette.co.uk

Summersdale Publishers Ltd
Part of Octopus Publishing Group Limited
Carmelite House
50 Victoria Embankment
LONDON
EC4Y 0DZ
UK

www.summersdale.com

Printed and bound in the Czech Republic

ISBN: 978-1-78783-327-2

Substantial discounts on bulk quantities of Summersdale books are available to corporations, professional associations and other organizations. For details contact general enquiries: telephone: +44 (0) 1243 771107 or email: enquiries@summersdale.com.

TO................................

FROM..............................

I LOVE
YOU MORE
THAN OTHER
HUMANS, BUT
LESS THAN
WINE AND
CATS.

ALL YOU
NEED IS
LOVE.
AND
LOVELY,
DISTRACTING
WI-FI.

I ATE A WHOLE
BUNCH OF LOVE
HEARTS TODAY AND
THOUGHT OF YOU.

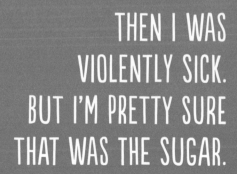

THEN I WAS
VIOLENTLY SICK.
BUT I'M PRETTY SURE
THAT WAS THE SUGAR.

I'd like to have
sex with you
until we achieve
a satisfactory
conclusion.

IF MY IMAGINARY FRIEND DOESN'T HATE YOU, **YOU'RE ALRIGHT BY ME.**

SNOG, MARRY, AVOID? WITH YOU, I'D LIKE TO DO ALL THREE.

WHEN I
WANT TO
CLOSE THE
DOOR ON
THE WORLD,
I'D LEAVE IT
SLIGHTLY
AJAR FOR
YOU.

YOU'RE THE
BEST THING TO
HAPPEN TO ME...

WE'RE THE WORST
THING TO HAPPEN
TO OTHER PEOPLE.

You've got everything I want on my ideal partner list. My heavily revised list.

YOU ARE
THE 40-WATT
BULB

**THAT LIGHTS
UP MY DAY.**

WE'RE LESS *WHEN HARRY MET SALLY*, MORE "WHEN VADER MET SAURON".

I'M GLAD
I GAVE
YOU MY
REAL
PHONE
NUMBER.

MY LOVE FOR
YOU IS REAL...

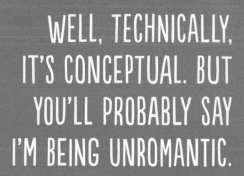

WELL, TECHNICALLY, IT'S CONCEPTUAL. BUT YOU'LL PROBABLY SAY I'M BEING UNROMANTIC.

Let's get a
takeaway
and bang.

I SMELL YOUR HAIR WHEN YOU'RE SLEEPING.

HARD NOT TO WHEN IT'S MATTED AGAINST MY FACE.

I ACTUALLY
USED TO
**HATE-
FOLLOW**
YOU ON
SOCIAL
MEDIA.

MY NUMBER
THREE PRIORITY
IN LIFE IS YOUR
HAPPINESS.
NUMBER ONE IS
MY HAMSTER'S
HAPPINESS;
NUMBER TWO
IS HAVING
ENOUGH
COFFEE.

I'LL LOVE YOU
UNTIL THE END
OF TIME.

HEY, LOOK — AT THE
END OF TIME YOU'LL
FINALLY HAVE YOUR
SHIT TOGETHER!

You own my
heart. And,
apparently,
most of my
favourite PJs.

LOVE IS
BEING TOO
STUBBORN

**TO SAY
YOU'RE
SORRY.**

THE JOY YOU BRING vs YOUR JACKHAMMER SNORING IS A CHOICE I MAKE EVERY DAY.

MY
**PERFECT
MORNING**
IS WAKING
UP BESIDE
YOU AND
BEATING
YOU TO THE
SHOWER.

WE COULD GET A DOG...

BUT I'VE ONLY GOT THE
CAPACITY TO NOT HATE
ONE THING AT A TIME.

My ex called
themselves the
tickle monster.
I love that
you'd never pull
that crap.

IT WASN'T
LOVE AT
FIRST SIGHT.

BUT, YEARS
LATER, WE'RE
GETTING
THERE.

IF WE EVER
BROKE UP,
I'D NOTICE
AND BE
**LESS THAN
HAPPY.**

I DON'T
NEED MY
DREAM LOVER.
I'M TOTALLY
OVER THE FACT
YOU DON'T
RIDE A HORSE.
TOTALLY.
OVER IT.

I WILL LOVE YOU
UNTIL DEATH...

THEN I'LL LISTEN TO
YOUR RECORDS, WEAR
YOUR T-SHIRTS AND
GET ON WITH THE
WEARISOME TASK OF
REPLACING YOU.

I require you.

ABSENCE MAKES THE HEART GROW FONDER.

AND THE HOME FEEL BIGGER.

WAS I LOST IN YOUR EYES? NO, SORRY – I JUST ZONED OUT FOR A BIT.

I SEE YOU
HACKED
ANOTHER
HAIRBALL
INTO THE
PLUGHOLE
THIS
MORNING.

WHEN WE'RE OLD AND
GREY, WE'LL BE ABLE TO
LOOK BACK AND SAY...

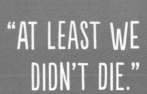

"AT LEAST WE
DIDN'T DIE."

I admire how
your rope-a-
dope dating
wore me
right down.

BECAUSE OF
YOU I HATE
ONE FEWER
THAN THE

**BILLIONS
OF PEOPLE
ON EARTH.**

WE'VE GOT SO MANY **MEMORIES** WITH YOUR FRIENDS. SOME OF THEM ARE **EVEN GOOD**.

YOU ARE MY ROCK: BOTH EMOTIONALLY AND IN TERMS OF TRYING TO ROLL YOU BACK TO YOUR SIDE OF THE BED.

MY LOVE FOR YOU
IS ENDLESS.

LIKE ROLLING NEWS
COVERAGE, BUT MUCH
LESS DEPRESSING.

You had me at "We're not getting any younger."

LOVE
FAVOURS
THE BRAVE.

**AND YOU
ARE VERY,
VERY BRAVE.**

I FELT THE EARTH MOVE LAST NIGHT. THE TYPICAL AFTERMATH OF CURRY NIGHT.

WE HATE
ALL THE
SAME
THINGS.

IF WE WERE STRANDED ON A DESERT ISLAND...

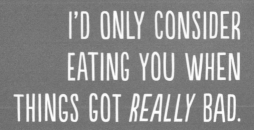

I'D ONLY CONSIDER
EATING YOU WHEN
THINGS GOT *REALLY* BAD.

Our love is
priceless. I
did put it on
eBay but they
made me take
it down.

I WAS
MENTALLY
SETTLED AS
A SPINSTER,

**BUT THIS IS
MUCH NICER.**

I LOVE
YOU MORE
THAN YOUR
MANY,
MANY,
MANY
FAULTS.

I WOULDN'T SAY YOU MAKE MY HEART SKIP BUT, SOMETIMES, YOU DO MAKE IT TWITCH.

YOU ARE THE
REASON I WAKE UP
IN THE MORNING...

YOU AND YOUR
STUPID SNOOZE
BUTTON.

Love can
transform an
enemy into
someone you
can tolerate.

YOU GET ME
HOT UNDER
THE COLLAR.

LIKE
MALARIA,
BUT IN A
NICE WAY.

YOU GIVE ME LIFE. LIKE A SEXY IRON LUNG.

YOU MAKE
OTHER
PEOPLE
SEEM EVEN
MORE
TIRESOME.

I DIDN'T BELIEVE
IN FAIRY TALES
UNTIL WE MET.

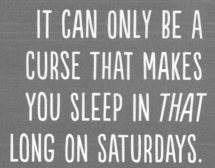

IT CAN ONLY BE A CURSE THAT MAKES YOU SLEEP IN *THAT* LONG ON SATURDAYS.

Love conquers
all. It wracks,
ruins and runs
off with the
village folk.

DINNER WITH YOUR PARENTS IS LIKE GOING TO IKEA:

ONE EYE ON THE MEATBALLS, ONE EYE TRYING TO FIND THE EXIT.

LIFE **WITHOUT YOU** IS EMPTY. LIFE **WITH YOU** IS BETTER THAN EMPTY.

YOU MAKE ME HAPPY. JUST.

I CAN'T PICTURE MY
LIFE WITHOUT YOU.

THEN AGAIN, I CAN'T PICTURE WHAT THE SOFA WOULD LOOK LIKE ON THE OTHER SIDE OF THE LIVING ROOM.

If you became homeless, I'd let you sleep in my garden.

I DON'T
NEED A
HOLLYWOOD
STAR, A
SUCCESSFUL
CAREERIST,
OR SOMEONE
COMPETENT.

**BECAUSE I
HAVE *YOU*.**

IF I COULD
REARRANGE
THE ALPHABET
I'D PUT "U" AND
"I" A COUPLE
OF LETTERS
CLOSER.

I WOULDN'T CHANGE MORE THAN **FOUR THINGS** ABOUT YOU.

MY SUPERPOWER WOULD BE SUPER-STRENGTH.

YOURS WOULD BE
INVISIBILITY, ACTIVATED
WHEN THE HOUSE
NEEDS CLEANING.

If I had a rose
for every time I
thought of you
I'd be pricked by
thorns all day.

HOLD MY
BODY, MY
BEER

AND MY
GRUDGES.

HAVING
YOU MAKES
QUEUES
AND
AIRPORT
LOUNGES
LESS DULL.

YOU ARE THE
AIR I BREATHE.
YOU ALSO
FREQUENTLY
TAINT THAT AIR.

I LOVE THAT I
CAN BE MYSELF
WITH YOU.

I'VE NEVER BEEN
ABLE TO EXPRESS
DISAPPOINTMENT
SO OPENLY.

I don't know
if it's impossible
to like you more,
or if it's just too
much effort.

MY LOVE FOR
YOU IS SO
DEEP THAT
IF I BURIED A
BODY THERE

**NOBODY
WOULD EVER
FIND IT.**

INSTEAD OF TOSSING THE CRAPPY CHOCOLATES, I SAVE THEM FOR YOU.

NOW I
ONLY
**SWIPE
RIGHT**
WHEN
WE PLAY
BADMINTON.

IT'S LIKE YOU'VE PUT A SPELL ON ME.

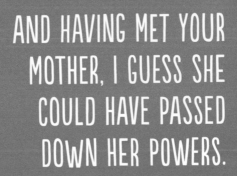

AND HAVING MET YOUR
MOTHER, I GUESS SHE
COULD HAVE PASSED
DOWN HER POWERS.

True love is eternal. Like some of your anecdotes.

YOU'RE LIKE
COMING
HOME –

MY PLACE TO
WIPE MY FEET
AND SLEEP.

NOBODY
LIKES **MY**
SARCASM
LIKE YOU
DO.

I REALLY
FANCY YOU.
AND IT'S
GETTING
WORSE.

I WAS TOLD I'D HAVE TO KISS A LOT OF FROGS UNTIL I FOUND "THE ONE".

I'D SAY YOU'RE LESS
"THE ONE", MORE LIKE
THE BEST FROG.

I love watching
you fall asleep.
Aaaaand on go
my cold feet.

I LOVE WHEN
WE CLOSE
THE DOOR.

**QUALITY
BITCH-
ABOUT-OUR-
FRIENDS
TIME.**

WHEN WE DO IT, I HAVE TO PINCH YOU SO YOU KNOW YOU'RE NOT DREAMING.

WHEN LIFE
GAVE ME
A LEMON, I
DATED YOU.

IF YOU LIVE TO BE
A HUNDRED, I WANT
TO BE A HUNDRED
MINUS ONE WEEK...

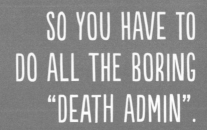

SO YOU HAVE TO
DO ALL THE BORING
"DEATH ADMIN".

I knew it was
real when the
beer goggles
came off and I
still thought: yes.

LOVE IS
INEXPLICABLE.

OURS
ESPECIALLY.

AT THE
MOMENT
I DON'T
REGRET
THIS.

I LOVE THAT WHEN WE GET A WEDDING INVITE FROM OUR FRIENDS WE GROAN IN PERFECT HARMONY.

A COLLEAGUE ASKED
ME TO DESCRIBE YOU
IN ONE WORD.

AFTER MUCH THOUGHT,
I SAID: "SCREW
YOU. I'M NOT A
PERFORMING MONKEY."

I know in my
heart that I
settled for the
right person.

WE'RE
JOINED
BY THE
GREATEST
BOND
THERE IS:

**A MORTGAGE.
I MEAN: LOVE.**

I WROTE IN YOUR CARD THAT YOU "CONSUME MY WHOLE BEING" BUT IT KINDA MAKES YOU SOUND LIKE SATAN.

I DON'T
ACTIVELY
HATE YOU.

MY HEART NO LONGER
BELONGS TO ME.

♥

I JUST SIGNED UP TO
BE AN ORGAN DONOR!

If loving you
was a job,
I'd do it for
minimum wage.

IT'S GOOD
YOU'RE
ALWAYS
THERE.

I'VE
ALIENATED
EVERYONE
ELSE.

I'VE MISSED
YOU SO
MUCH I
WISH TO
GIVE YOU
**BIG, NEEDY
SQUEEZES**.

WILL HATE
LESS FOR
BACK RUBS.

WE'RE BOTH GUILTY OF
A CRIMINAL OFFENCE:
YOU STOLE MY HEART
AND I STOLE YOURS.

AND WE STOLE THOSE
FLUFFY DRESSING GOWNS
FROM THAT HOTEL.

I'll always love
you. Or, to
cover myself
legally: I'll
always *try*.

GOD, YOU'RE
SEXILY

ANNOYING.

ONCE IN
A WHILE,
SOMETHING
AMAZING
COMES
ALONG. OH,
HERE I AM!

LOVE IS
COMPOSED
OF A
**SINGLE
MILD
HATRED**
INHABITING
TWO BODIES.

THANKS FOR BEING
THERE FOR ME EVEN
WHEN I DON'T
DESERVE IT.

WHICH, LET'S BE
HONEST, IS A LOT.

Let's flip a coin:
heads, I'm yours.
Tails, you're
the designated
driver this
weekend.

WHEN YOU'RE NOT AT HOME I FEEL LOST.

MAYBE I COULD FIND MY WAY AROUND IF YOU TIDIED AWAY YOUR CRAP.

I LOVE
EVERY PART
OF YOUR
BODY.
WELL, APART
FROM YOUR
FEET.

YOU ARE
MY SUN IN
THE BLEAK
UNIVERSE
THAT IS
OTHER
PEOPLE.

YOU'RE LIKE MY
BAG FOR LIFE...

DURABLE, A GOOD
CAUSE AND IF I RUIN
YOU HOPEFULLY I'LL BE
GIVEN ANOTHER ONE.

I wished on a star and, the day after, I met you. Incidentally, my wish never came true.

WE'RE LIKE PUZZLE PIECES.

OUR JAGGED EDGES JUST MATCH UP.

YOU'RE LIKE MY LITTLE PUSSY CAT: ALOOF, OBSESSED WITH FOOD AND YOU AVOID THE VACUUM CLEANER.

YOU DON'T
COMPLETE
ME BUT
YOU'RE
CERTAINLY
**A HANDY
ADDITION**.

I WOULDN'T SAY
YOU'RE A HOARDER.

AT LEAST THEY LEAVE
ENOUGH SPACE TO GET
IN THE FRONT DOOR.

Our love is
unpredictable.
Like when you
creep up behind
a horse.

I'M GLAD

YOU'RE
STILL HERE.

YOU'RE
A MUCH
BETTER
PERSON
FOR
**KNOWING
ME.**

YOU'RE
SO SUGARY,
SYRUPY AND
SWEET –
EVERYTHING
MY DENTIST
WARNED ME
ABOUT.

I DON'T NEED
A BIG HOUSE OR
A FANCY CAR.

BUT I DO NEED
YOU TO NOT LEAVE
NAIL CLIPPINGS ON
THE WORKTOP.

I love you
unconditionally.
But for the love
of god, your
laundry basket...

YOU MAKE
ME WANT
TO HISS AT

**ANYONE
WHO LOOKS
AT YOU.**

I'D LIKE YOU
TO ANNOY
ME FOR THE
FORESEEABLE
FUTURE.

NOT ALL
**DRUNKEN
MISTAKES**
ARE
REGRETS.

MY LOVE IS LIKE AN OCEAN.

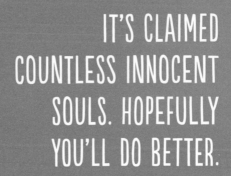

IT'S CLAIMED
COUNTLESS INNOCENT
SOULS. HOPEFULLY
YOU'LL DO BETTER.

There's nothing
I wouldn't
do for you.
Within reason.

YOU MAKE
ME FEEL
ALIVE. LET'S
NOT WASH
FOR A WEEK

AND GO
TRY ON
EVERYTHING
IN RALPH
LAUREN.

YOU
CANNOT
ESCAPE
THE **BLACK
HOLE** OF
MY LOVE.

I'LL NEVER LEAVE YOUR SIDE. UNLESS YOU'RE IN THE TOILET. OR HOLDING A SNAKE.

I ENJOYED
THE THRILL OF
THE CHASE...

BUT NOT AS MUCH
AS WHEN MY LION
FINALLY HAULED DOWN
YOUR GAZELLE.

If I could turn
back the
clock, I'd have
stopped sucking
in my stomach
much sooner.

I HATE YOU

THE LEAST.

If you're interested in finding out more about our books, find us on Facebook at **Summersdale Publishers** and follow us on Twitter at **@Summersdale**.

www.summersdale.com